Environmental Lifestyle Guide

For Grade 10 Students

VOL.5 OF 11

Cleaning

Jahangir Asadi

Vancouver, BC CANADA

Published by: Silosa Consulting Group Inc.
Vancouver, BC **CANADA**
Email: Info@Silosa.ca
www.silosa.ca

Ordering Information:
Quantity sales. Special discounts are available on quantity purchases by universities, schools, corporations, associations, and others. For details, contact the "Sales Department" at the above mentioned email address.

Environmental lifestyle Guide Vol.5 for Grade.10/J.Asadi —1st ed.
ISBN: 978-1-990451-79-9

Contents

We hope that, 10,000 years from now, future generations will be able to see flowers that provide bees with nectar and pollen and...
BEES provide flowers with the means to reproduce by spreading pollen from flower to flower,....

Jahangir Asadi

This book is dedicated to my professor, Dr.Bijan Esfandiari

Introduction

This book is part of an eleven volume series that is meant to be a standard textbook series, for grades 9 to 12. TTAIN & ESFK & SCG improves quality of life and reduces environmental degradation by fostering new consumption patterns and sustainable lifestyles through International Cooperative Extension Service programs at houses, offices, schools and libraries all over the globe.

Climate change is real. Therefore people have the potential to make a difference now and for future generations. This book provides climate science basics, including the roles that lifestyles and populations play in the climate scenario, the significance of carbon footprints, and an overview of the current climate situation. The manual has been categorized based on humanity's needs starting first with food and ending with tourism. The manual then illustrates the difference between adaptation (taking steps to live with the changes) and mitigation (taking steps to slow the rate of change.)

Adaptation examples include food, energy, transportation, recreation. Mitigation focuses on effectively engaging with local governments, through serving on advisory boards, communicating with public officials, educational institutes, schools, universities, libraries and leading communities towards climate change actions.

One useful way to mitigate climate change is through increasing public knowledge to better understand the impact of the rate of change on plants and animals. This is crucial for preserving species; and for assessing potential insects and disease outbreaks in agriculture, natural resources and public health.

Taking personal action is a key element of this manual.

Citizens are challenged to consume 20% fewer resources, to bring world consumption levels down as much as possible. Readers are given 12 practical steps to take to make the changes. The resources section provides additional information, and readers are encouraged to contact the author for further questions.

As an accessibility action, we have provided Online international courses on climate change control as well. You can access the courses via the following link:

http://TopTenAward.org

SILOSA Consulting Group (SCG)

Silosa Consulting Group (SCG) was established to provide outstanding consulting services of management system & educational standards to individuals, groups, companies, schools, and organizations all over the globe. SCG is publishing an "Environmental Lifestyle Guide " book series as a standard textbook related to increasing environmental awareness of students means being aware of the natural environment and making choices that benefit the earth, rather than hurt it. Vol.1 to 11 (for grades 9 to 12) providing some of the ways to practice environmental awareness include: **Recycling**, **Conserving energy and water**, **Reuse, Activism, and others**.

SCG book publishing services and distribution services are connected to over 39,000 booksellers worldwide, including Apple, Amazon, Barnes & Noble, Indigo, Google Play Books, and many more. SCG has enough experiences to help create new and effective environmental educational programmes in different countries all over the world. For more detail, visit our website : http://silosa.ca and/or send your enquirer to the following email:

info@silosa.ca

CHAPTER 1

About ISO 14000 for Students

The International Organization for Standardization is an independent, non-governmental organization, the members of which are the standards organizations of the 165 member countries. It is the world's largest developer of voluntary international standards and it facilitates world trade by providing common standards among nations. More than twenty thousand standards have been set, covering everything from manufactured products and technology to food safety, agriculture, and healthcare.

Kids ISO 14000s
"Kids ISO 14000s" is a new environmental education program for children, based on ISO 14000s, which is international standard for environmental management. Primary aims of this program are: -
1. To teach and train children how to manage the environmental issues (such as energy saving) by themselves through the working book and guide book of this program,
2. To certify those children who showed good accomplishment in the program from highly international authority (as is the case of ISO 14000s)
3. To network those children through the international network (Kids International Network), so that the children can work on the environment, internationally.

2. System of Kids ISO 14000s Program

The system of Kids ISO 14000s Program consists of

1. Operation Headquarter (ArTech).

2. Workbook, Guidebook (originally published by ArTech, and local versions are produced by each countries).

3. Eco-Kids-Instructors for local operation and evaluation of the performance of the children.

4. International accreditation committee for accreditation of accomplishment of the children, for certification of the Eco-Kids-Instructors, as well as overall checks of this program.

5. Linkage with international organizations (such as UNU, UNESCO, etc. …) And also national organizations

More information can be obtained :

www.ISO.org

Canada

Environmental Sustain for Future kids established in Vancouver, BC Canada in 2020. (ESFK) is an international ecolabel focused on taking care of environment for future of kids. ESFK defined as 'self-declared' environmental claims made by manufacturers and businesses based on ISO 14020 series of standards, the claimant can declare the environmental objectives and targets in relation to taking care of environment for future kids. However, this declaration will be verifiable.

Environmental Sustain for Future Kids
Vancouver, BC CANADA

Email: info@esfk.org
Web: www.esfk.org

STEP FIVE

All about 'Eco-friendly' Cleaning Products

G reen cleaning products should not contain hazardous chemicals, and so they are likely to pose fewer health risks. Green cleaning products are less hazardous for the environment, too. They do not contain chemicals that cause significant air or water pollution and are often in recyclable or recycled packaging. The eco-friendly cleaning products, also known as green cleaning products, are made from plant-based ingredients, natural colors or fragrances, uses eco-friendly packaging methods, and are biodegradable. Support sustainable human and ecological use and reuse of remediated land; Minimize impacts to water quality and water resources; Reduce air toxics emissions and greenhouse gas production; Minimize material use and waste production; and Conserve natural resources and energy.

How do I know which cleaning products are the most environmentally friendly?

Almost all people from all over the world use household cleaning products from dish detergents to bathroom cleaners and floor polish to scouring pads. Most of us are exposed to cleaners on a daily basis,... Even if we don't use cleaners, it's likely we're regularly come into contact with them at work, school or elsewhere.

Unfortunately, cleaners often contain harsh chemicals that can be harmful to our health and planet. Health effects associated with cleaning products include asthma, contact dermatitis, burns to the skin and eyes and inflammation or fluid in the lungs. Long-term repercussions may include reproductive problems, cancer, heart disease and other health issues. The environment also can fall victim to cleaning products' acrid ingredients. Chemicals in laundry detergents, for example, have been found in 75 percent of streams

and waterways throughout in different countries. Some ingredients in cleaners have been directly linked to environmental problems, such as chemicals getting into bodies of water and foaming in streams, and some commonly used household cleaner ingredients have room for improvement even today. Health and environmental concerns have prompted many consumers to push for safer alternatives to cleaning products. **But identifying environmentally safe cleaners can be challenging for consumers.** With so many product options, choosing the safest, healthiest cleaners for the home can be challenging for reasons other than too many choices, namely the lack of a national regulatory body. A fraction of the tens of thousands of chemicals in commerce in different countries are used in consumer goods like household cleaners. Chemicals are regulated as they enter commerce rather than at the product level.

But shoppers who want to know exact ingredients might not find what they're looking for on household cleaner labels. In many countries law does not require manufacturers of cleaning products to list all ingredients on labels. But manufacturers might be changing their ways in the near future. Some of the associations, launched a joint, voluntary effort to encourage their members to list their ingredients in a public format. In the meantime, consumers are left to make sense of what's on the packaging.

Different manufacturers can make the same marketing claim like "degradable" or "ozone-friendly" and mean different things with those terms. This has resulted in confusion among consumers.

Besides looking for the Design for Environment Labellings and knowing what marketing terms mean, consumers can also read product packaging to make sure environmental claims are qualified. All assertions should specify whether it's referring to the product, packaging or both. Similarly, Environmental labels should come with an explanation and identify the third party doing the certifying.

The organization should be independent from advertisers and have expertise in the area for which it's certifying. Other indicators of environmental responsibility are the following: recycled, recyclable or refillable containers; concentrated products that require less packaging; cleaners free of chlorofluorocarbons (CFCs) that can deplete the ozone; and degradable, biodegradable or photodegradable product contents or packaging.

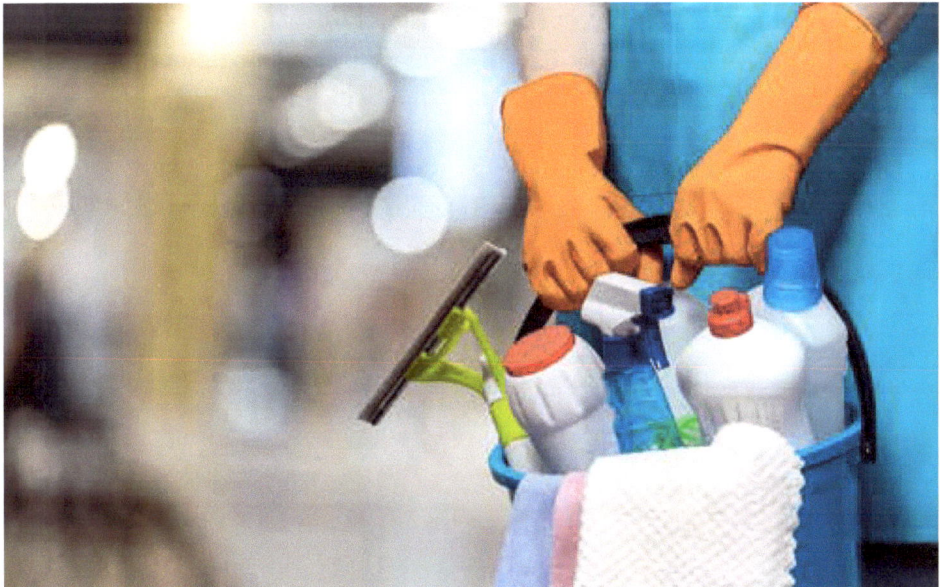

For example, a toilet cleaner ad that claims the solid waste generated by disposing of its container is "now 20 percent less than our previous container," is in good practice if the cleaner company can prove disposal of the new package contributes 20 percent less waste by weight or volume to the solid waste stream. Comparatively, the general claim "20 percent less waste" is ambiguous and therefore deceptive because it's unclear if the claim is referring to a preceding product or that of a competitor, according to the general principles on International Environmental labelling.

Homemade Cleaning Products: Natural, Green, Eco-Friendly

A mixture of vinegar and baking soda can do wonders for your cleaning needs. This combination can be used in many ways to fight against severe stains, so you do not need to run out to the grocery store to buy a solution filled with chemicals anymore. Not only will natural cleaners make your life better, they will virtually eliminate that bad smell in the house and they're surprisingly inexpensive to create.

Chemical - free Recipes for Homemade Cleaning Products:

If you're wanting to pitch those toxic, commercial household cleaners and switch to natural, homemade cleaner, these simple recipes will have you cleaning green in no time, Before we get to the cleaning, let's check out some of the most common (and most useful) non-toxic cleaning products:

Baking Soda
Baking soda is a pantry staple with proven virus-killing abilities that also effectively cleans, deodorizes, brightens, and cuts through grease and grimeTrusted Source.

Castile Soap
Castile soap is a style of soap that's made from 100 percent plant oils (meaning it uses no animal products or chemical detergents).

Vinegar
Thanks to its acidity, vinegar is nothing short of a cleaning wunderkind—it effectively (and gently!) eliminates grease, soap scum, and grime.

Lemon Juice
Natural lemon juice annihilates mildew and mold, cuts through grease, and shines hard surfaces (It also smells awesome.).

Olive Oil
This good-for-you cooking oil also works as a cleaner and polisher.

Essential Oils
Essential oils have gained popularity thanks to aromatherapy, but these naturally occurring plant compounds also make great scent additions to homemade cleaning products (particularly if you're not into the smell of vinegar). Essential oils are generally considered safe, but these extracts can trigger allergies—so keep this in mind when choosing scents.

Borax

Many DIY cleaners tout Borax (a boron mineral and salt) as a non-toxic alternative to mainstream cleaning products; however, the issue is pretty hotly debated. Some research suggests Borax can act as a skin and eye irritant and that it disrupts hormones. For this list, we've chosen to avoid products that use Borax.

A note on mixing products:

Most of these ingredients can be used in combination with each other; however, many sources advise against mixing castile soap with vinegar or lemon juice. Since castile soap is basic (i.e., high on the pH scale) and vinegar and lemons are acidic, the products basically cancel each other out when used in combination (though it's fine to wash with a base—like castille soap—and rinse with an acid—like vinegar!).

Cleaning Recipes

Many of these cleaners can be used in multiple places, but we've assigned them to particular areas for easy reference:

- **Bathroom**
- **Kitchen**
- **Lundry Room**
- **Others**

Bathroom

1. Toilets

For a heavy-duty toilet scrub that deodorizes while it cleans, pour ½ cup of baking soda and about 10 drops of tea tree essential oil into the toilet. Add ¼ cup of vinegar to the bowl and scrub away while the mixture fizzes.

For daily cleaning, fill a small spray bottle with vinegar (about 1 cup should do it) and a few drops of an essential oil of your choosing (lemon and tea tree both work well). Spray on the toilet seats, let it sit for a few minutes, and then wipe the surface clean.

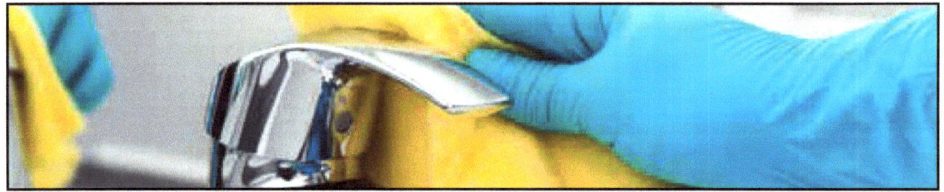

2. Tub and Shower

Tubs and showers can produce some of the toughest grime, but it's no match for the cleaning power of vinegar. To get rid of mildew, spray pure white vinegar on the offending area, let it sit for at least 30 minutes, and then rinse with warm water (don't be afraid to use a sponge if rinsing doesn't clear away the grossness on its own). Alternatively, try mixing together baking soda with a bit of liquid castile soap, then scrub and rinse.

For daily cleaning or to get rid of soap scum, mix 1 part water with 1 part vinegar (and a few drops of essential oils if you're not into the smell of vinegar) in a spray bottle. Spray, let it sit for at least several minutes, and then wipe away.

3. Disinfectant
Skip the bleach and make a homemade germ-killer instead. Just mix 2 cups of water, 3 tablespoons of liquid soap, and 20-30 drops of tea tree oil. Voila!

4. Air Freshener
Defeat less-visible bathroom "uncleanliness" with this homemade, non-toxic air freshener. All you need is baking soda, your favorite essential oil, and an old jar with a lid you don't mind poking holes in (follow the link for full instructions).

5. Hand Soap
Once you're done cleaning the bathroom, it's time to make yourself clean (or at least your hands). To make a non-toxic, foaming hand soap, mix together liquid castile soap and water (and an essential oil if you feel like it) in a foaming soap dispenser. Fill about one fifth of the bottle with soap, then top it off with water.

Kitchen

6-Countertops

For a simple, all-purpose counter cleaner, mix together equal parts vinegar and water in a spray bottle. If your countertop is made from marble, granite, or stone, skip the vinegar (its acidity is no good for these surfaces) and use rubbing alcohol or the wondrous power of vodka instead.

7. Cutting Boards

Talk about non-toxic: All that's needed to clean and sanitize cutting boards (wood or plastic) is… a lemon! Cut it in half, run it over the surfaces, let sit for ten minutes, and then rinse away. If you need some serious scrubbing power, sprinkle some coarse or Kosher salt over the board, and then rub with ½ a lemon.

8. Oven

To clean stubborn, caked-on food out of the oven, just heat the over to 125 degrees and grab your spray bottle of vinegar (see "countertops" above). Once the oven is warm, spray the caked-on stuff until it's lightly damp and then pour salt directly onto the affected areas. Turn off the oven, let it cool, and then use a wet towel to scrub away at the mess. If that doesn't cut it, follow the same instructions but try use baking soda in place of salt (just let it sit for a few minutes before scrubbing).

9. Garbage Disposal

This one is so cool. Pour 1 cup of vinegar into an ice cube tray and top off the slots with water. Once they're frozen, toss a few down the disposal and let it run—doing so should remove any food that was stuck to the blades.

10. Microwave

It's easy to overlook the microwave while cleaning, but man can it get gross in there. To combat the gunk, pour some vinegar into a small cup and mix in a little lemon juice (exact amounts don't really matter). Put the cup in the microwave, let the microwave run for 2 minutes, and leave the door closed for several more minutes. Finally, open the door and simply wipe down all the sides with a warm cloth or sponge—no scrubbing required!

11. Sink Drain

To unclog a stuffed-up drain, start by boiling about 2 cups of water. Pour ½ cup of baking soda into the drain, and then add the water while it's still nice and hot. If that doesn't do the trick, follow the baking soda with ½ cup of vinegar, cover it up tightly (a pot lid should work nicely), wait until the fizzing slows down (when baking soda and vinegar come in contact, they'll react by fizzing) and then add one gallon of boiling water.

12. Pan De-Greaser

To cut through the grime on frying pans, simply apply some salt (no water necessary) and scrub vigorously.

13. Cast-Iron Pans

Kitchen professionals are pretty against using soap, steel wool, or dishwashers to clean cast-iron pans. Luckily, there's an alternative way to tackle cast-iron grossness: combine olive oil and a teaspoon of coarse salt in the pan. Scrub with a stiff brush, rinse with hot water, and you're done!

14. Dishwasher Detergent

If you're lucky enough to have a dishwasher, simply mix together 1 cup of liquid castile soap and 1 cup of water (2 teaspoons of lemon juice optional) in a quart-size glass jar. Add some of this mixture to one detergent compartment of the dishwasher, and fill the other compartment with white vinegar.

15. Dish Soap
If washing dishes by hand, simply combine 1 cup of liquid castile soap and 3 tablespoons water (a few drops of essential oil optional) in a bottle of your choice. Shake well and use like you would any other dish soap.

16. Refrigerator Cleaner
To clean what is perhaps the toughest of all kitchen "gross spots," reach for the baking soda. Add about ½ cup of the white stuff to a bucket of hot water. Dip a clean rag in the mixture and use it to wipe down the fridge's insides.

17. Bleach
For serious disinfectant power, mix ½ cup baking soda, 1 teaspoon castile soap, and ½ teaspoon hydrogen peroxide. Use a cloth to apply the mixture to a wet surface, scrub, and then rinse thoroughly.

Lundry Room

18. Laundry Detergent
It's tough to come by homemade laundry detergents that don't use Borax, but give this one a try. The recipe calls for glycerin soap, washing soda, baking soda, citric acid, and coarse salt. For full instructions, follow the link!

19. Fabric Softener
Skip the liquid fabric softener and make clothes nice and snuggly the non-toxic way. Make a big batch of softener by adding 20-30 drops of the essential oil of your choice to a one-gallon jug of white vinegar. Add 1/3 cup to each laundry load (just be sure to shake the mixture prior to each use).

20. Laundry "Scenter"
To add a fresh, clean scent to laundry, make a sachet stuffed with your favorite dried herbs (lavender, peppermint, and lemon verbena are all great options). Toss it in the dryer while it's in use, and voila: customized, non-toxic scent!

21. Bleach
For a nontoxic laundry bleach alternative, add some lemon juice to the rinse cycle.

Everything Else

22. Floors
For a simple, effective tile floor cleaner, simply combine one part white vinegar with two parts warm water in a bucket. Use a mop or rag to scrub down the floors with the solution. No need to rinse off! (Note: this one's not recommended for wood floors).

23. Walls
To scrub down walls, mix ¼ cup white vinegar with 1 quart warm water, then use a rag to scrub those walls down. To remove black marks, simply scrub at the spot with a little bit of baking soda.

24. Windows and Mirrors
For an all-purpose window cleaner, combine 1 part white vinegar with 4 parts water (feel free to add some lemon juice if you're feeling citrusy), then use a sponge or rag to scrub away.

25. Furniture Polish
For an all-purpose furniture polish, combine ¼ cup vinegar with ¾ cup olive oil and use a soft cloth to distribute the mixture over furniture. For wood furniture (or as an alternative to the first recipe), combine ¼ cup lemon juice with ½ cup olive oil, then follow the same procedure.

26. Silver Cleaner

Put silver utensils and jewelry back to good use the non-toxic way. Line a sink or bucket with aluminum foil, lay out the silver on top of the aluminum, and pour in boiling water, 1 cup of baking soda, and a pinch of salt. Let it sit for several minutes and watch as—like magic—the tarnish disappears! Note: If you're concerned about immersing a particular item, simply rub it with toothpaste and a soft cloth, rinse it with warm water, and allow it air to dry.

27. Wood Cleaner

Clean varnished wood by combining 2 tablespoons of olive oil, 1 tablespoon of white vinegar, and a quart of warm water in a spray bottle. Spray onto wood and then dry with a soft cloth. (Note: Since olive oil can leave behind some (slippery) residue, this one might not be the best option for wood floors.)

Important Note: We've done our absolute best to provide the best information possible, but since we haven't tried every single one of these solutions in every possible cleaning situation, we can't vouch for them 100 percent.

What's the difference between products that disinfect, sanitize, and clean surfaces?

Products used to kill viruses and bacteria on surfaces are considered as antimicrobial pesticides. Sanitizers and disinfectants are two types of anti-microbial pesticides.

Cleaning	Cleaning removes dirt and organic matter from surfaces using soap or detergents.
Sanitizing	Sanitizing kills bacteria on surfaces using chemicals. It is not intended to kill viruses.
Disinfecting	Disinfecting kills viruses and bacteria on surfaces using chemicals.

Experts agree that frequent handwashing is one of the first lines of defense against many illnesses. But no matter how many times you wash your hands, there are always some sneaky little germs lurking around to hitch a ride on your skin. They loiter on shopping cart handles, linger on light switches, lurk about the phone and even hang around on the remote controls. That's why disinfectants and disinfecting cleaners can be a helpful option.

Why Disinfect
• Regular cleaning products do a good job of removing soil and many germs. Disinfectants or disinfectant cleaners are able to go further and kill many of those germs.
• Surfaces may be contaminated even when they're not visibly soiled.
• Germs can live on surfaces for hours or even days.

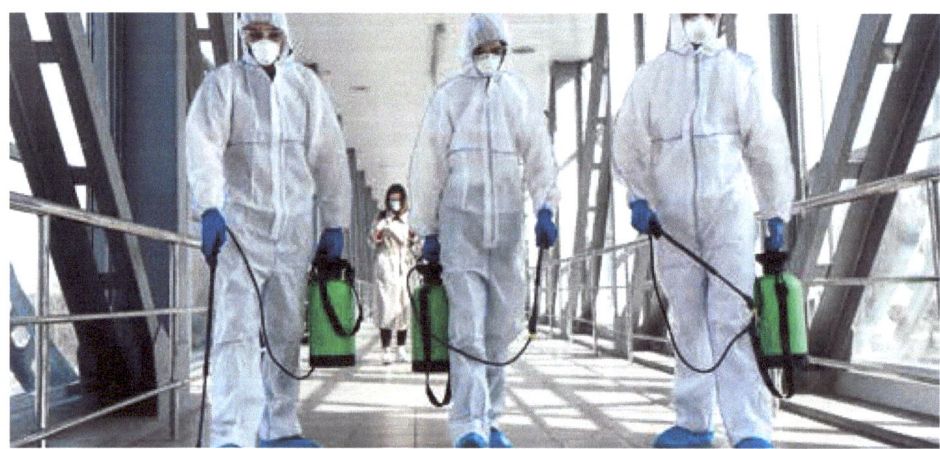

How to Disinfect

- Read the label before using any cleaning or disinfecting product to ensure you are following the directions for use and storage instructions.
- Pre-clean any surfaces prior to disinfecting to remove any excess dirt or grime.
- Apply the disinfectant, then the surface needs to stay wet for the entire time indicated on the product label; this is called contact time.
- If disinfecting food contact surfaces or toys, rinse with water after they air dry.
- When disinfecting, target surfaces that are frequently touched, especially if someone in the home is ill.
- If using a disinfectant wipe, throw out after using. Do not flush any non-flushable products.

What to Look for in a Disinfectant

Products that say "Disinfectant" on the label are required to meet legal specifications. To be sure the product has met all defined requirements for effectiveness, look for Registration Number on the label. You must follow the product label instructions exactly for the disinfectant to be effective. Your choices include:

Chlorine bleach. It disinfects when mixed and used properly. Read the label for instructions.

Disinfectant cleaners. These dual purpose products contain ingredients that help remove soil as well as kill germs.

Disinfectants. These products are designed to be effective against the germs indicated on their labels. Surfaces should be clean prior to disinfecting.

Some of the more frequently used active ingredients are sodium hypochlorite, ethanol, pine oil, hydrogen peroxide, citric acid and quats (quaternary ammonium compounds).

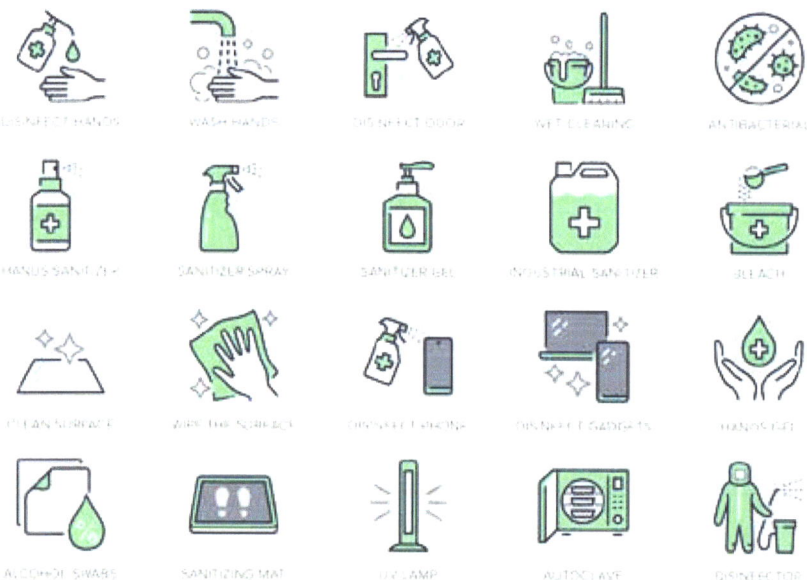

When killing surface germs is your goal, look for products that are disinfectants, some common disinfectants include Quaternary Ammonium Compounds (QACs), commonly referred to as Quats.

The Future of Cleaning

Cleaning technology has come a long way from the ancient Babylonian way of soap-making. Today's cleaning products are the result of thoughtful design, experimentation, and safety testing.

The machines we use to clean have also improved, becoming more sustainable and friendly for our environment. So far we have been able to make new cleaning products that allow us to wash in cold water (saving energy from water heating), wash with less water, and make packaging smaller (to save material and avoid shipping extra weight).

Future scientists will have a great opportunity to continue to create new cleaning design products that will continue to keep us healthy and do even more to help protect human health and the environment.

Nanotechnology is the future, not only for things like computers and building materials but also for cleaning products. Not only is it important to focus on keeping surface areas clean, but we should also keep in mind air quality.

Many workers have transitioned to more remote work over the past year, meaning more time spent inside your home with who knows what kind of germs or contaminants lingering. Some air-purification systems don't always catch pollutants at room temperature.

Nanotechnology aids in the filtration of such pollutants. Air-purifier sprays like Purbloc's NANO GRAB are your ticket to a clean, germ-free, home.

Harmful toxins leached out by ordinary household cleaners can cause everything from chapped hands to potential lung issues in the long term. Long-term health issues can then translate to high costs.

By going with a natural cleaner you're thinking of not only your long-term health, but you're saving money in the long run by taking care of yourself now and those around you with safe and effective supplies.

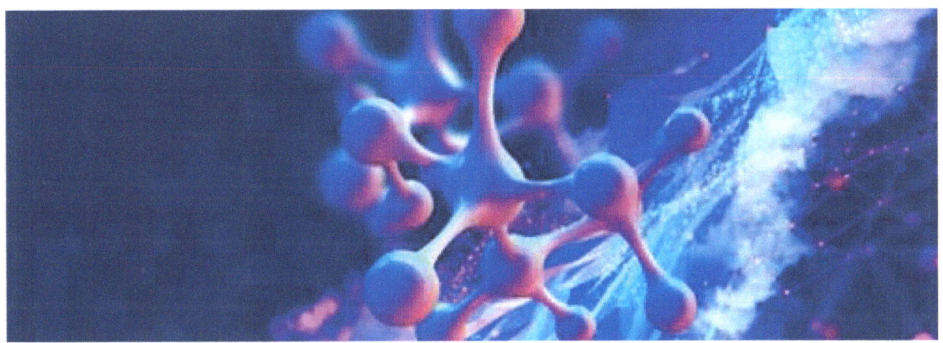

Keep in Mind

There are so many incredible real-world benefits of nanotechnology. A summation of a few products and processes enhanced by such benefits:

- Coatings to reduce cleaning efforts
- Improved energy efficiency
- Fabrics with increased resistance to stains
- Extra durable goods that increase the life of a product thus creating less waste in the long run
- Easier and more efficient water filtration
- Insulation materials reducing the energy needed to heat and cool buildings

Families and businesses alike can all benefit from the efficient uses mentioned above. From the reduction of energy consumption to the wonders of regenerative medicine, nanotechnology is a key player in the race toward enhancing and caring for our way of living.

What makes cleaning products eco-friendly?

Not containing toxic chemicals.
Has biodegradable ingredients.
Being made from plants.
Not using single use plastic.
Being plastic free entirely.
Being refillable.
Not creating waste.
Being vegan and/or cruelty free.

ECO HO

nature frie

SEHOLD
y products

CANADA SILVER BEAVER BADGE

Participate in our Online Classes to earn these exclusive digital badges!
www.toptenaward.org

Design & Development by:

Tara Asadi

1) If washing dishes by hand, simply combine _____ _____ of liquid castile soap and 3 tablespoons water in a bottle of your choice.
A) 1 cup
B) 1 bottle
C) 2 cups
D) 5 liter
ANSWER:

2) For serious disinfectant power, mix _____ _____ baking soda, 1 teaspoon castile soap, and ½ teaspoon hydrogen peroxide.
A) 1 cup
B) ½ cup
C) 2 cups
D) 5 liter
ANSWER:

3) Many DIY cleaners tout Borax as a non-toxic alternative to mainstream cleaning products; the issue is pretty hotly debated.
A) True
B) False
ANSWER:

4) _____ _____ should come with an explanation and identify the third party doing the certifying.
A) Economic analysis
B) Extra Bags
C) Environmental Labels
D) Recycle sign
ANSWER:

5) For a heavy-duty toilet scrub that deodorizes while it cleans, pour ½ cup of baking soda and about 10 drops of tea tree essential oil into the toilet. Spray on the toilet seats, let it sit for a few minutes, and then wipe the surface clean.
A) True
B) False
ANSWER:

6) Some research suggests Borax can act as a skin and eye irritant and that it disrupts hormones.
A) True
B) False
ANSWER:

7) Natural _____ _____ annihilates mildew and mold, cuts through grease, and shines hard surfaces.
A) Spring Water
B) Orange Juice
C) Baking Soda
D) Lemon Juice
ANSWER:

8) Doing so should remove any food that was stuck to the blades (Garbage Disposal), Pour _____ _____ of vinegar into an ice cube tray and top off the slots with water.
A) 1 cup
B) ½ cup
C) 2 cups
D) 5 liter
ANSWER:

9) Green cleaning products should not contain hazardous chemicals, and so they are likely to pose fewer health risks.
A) True
B) False
ANSWER:

10) Make a big batch of softener by adding 30-20 drops of the essential oil of your choice to a _____ jug of white vinegar.
A) 1 cup
B) 1 gallon
C) 2 cups
D) 5 liter
ANSWER:

11) For daily cleaning or to get rid of soap scum, mix 1 part water with 1 part vinegar in a spray bottle.
A) True
B) False
ANSWER:

12) For daily cleaning, fill a small spray bottle with vinegar and a few drops of an essential oil of your choosing.
A) True
B) False
ANSWER:

13) Green cleaning products are less hazardous for the environment, too.
A) True
B) False
ANSWER:

14)Cleaning Furniture, combine _____ lemon juice. with _____ olive oil, then follow the same procedure.
A) ¼ cup, ½ cup
B) 1 cup, ½ cup
C) ½ cup, ½ cup
D) ¼ cup, 1 cup
ANSWER:

15) The eco-friendly cleaning products, also known as green cleaning products, are made from plant-based ingredients, natural colors or fragrances, uses eco-friendly packaging methods, and are biodegradable.
A) True
B) False
ANSWER:

16) In many countries law does not require manufacturers of _____ _____ to list all ingredients on labels.
A) Bleaching liquids
B) cleaning products
C) dishwashers' liquids
D) Hair Shampoo
ANSWER:

17) For daily cleaning or to get rid of soap scum, mix 1 part water with 1 part vinegar in a spray bottle. Spray, let it sit for at least several minutes, and then wipe away.
A) True
B) False
ANSWER:

18) To make a non-toxic, foaming _____ _____, mix together liquid castile soap and water in a foaming soap dispenser.
A) Bleaching liquids
B) hand soap
C) dishwashers' liquids
D) Hair Shampoo
ANSWER:

19) Clean varnished wood by combining 2 tablespoons of olive oil, 1 tablespoon of white vinegar, and a quart of warm water in a spray bottle.
A) True
B) False
ANSWER:

20) To combat the gunk, pour some vinegar into a small cup and mix in a little lemon juice.
A) True
B) False
ANSWER:

21) Refrigerator Cleaner: To clean what is perhaps the toughest of all kitchens "gross spots," reach for the baking soda. Add about ____ of the white stuff to a bucket of hot water. Dip a clean rag in the mixture and use it to wipe down the fridge's insides.
A) 1 cup
B) ½ cup
C) 2 cups
D) 5 liter
ANSWER:

22) Bleach: For serious disinfectant power, mix ½ cup baking soda, 1 teaspoon castile soap, and ½ teaspoon hydrogen peroxide. Use a cloth to apply the mixture to a wet surface, scrub, and then rinse thoroughly.
A) True
B) False
ANSWER:

23)For a heavy-duty toilet scrub that deodorizes while it cleans, pour ½ cup of baking soda and about 10 drops of tea tree essential oil into the toilet.
A) True
B) False
ANSWER:

24) Green cleaning products should not contain hazardous chemicals, and so they are likely to pose fewer health risks.
A) True
B) False
ANSWER:

25) For serious disinfectant power, mix ½ cup baking soda, 1 teaspoon castile soap, and ½ teaspoon hydrogen peroxide.
A) True
B) False
ANSWER:

Bibliography:

Amberg, N.; Magda, R. Environmental Pollution and Sustainability or the Impact of the Environmentally Conscious Measures of International Cosmetic Companies on Purchasing Organic Cosmetics. Visegrad J. Bioecon. Sustain. Dev. 2018, 1, 23.

Asadi, J., "International Environmental Labelling, Economic Consequencies, Export Magazine, July 2001

Asadi, J. 2008. Mobile Phone as management systems tools, ISO Magazine, Vol.8, No.1

Asadi, J., Eco-Labelling Standards, National Standard Magazine, Sep. 2004.

Barbieux, D.; Padula, A.D. Paths and Challenges of New Technologies: The Case of Nanotechnology-Based Cosmetics Development in Brazil. Adm. Sci. 2018, 8, 16.

Basketter, D.; Corsini, E. Can We Make Cosmetic Contact Allergy History? Cosmetics 2016, 3, 11.

Benitta Christy P & Dr. Kavitha S, "GO-GREEN TEXTILES FOR ENVIRONMENT", Advanced Engineering and Applied Sciences: An International Journal 2014; 4(3): 26-28

Chemical Week, 1999. Europe's Beef Ban Tests Precautionary Principle. (August 11).

Chaudri, S.K.; Jain, N.K. History of Cosmetics. Asian J. Pharm. 2009, 7–9, 164–167.

CHOI, J.P. Brand Extension as Informational Leverage. Review of Eco- nomic Studies, Vol. 65 (1998), pp. 655-669.

Conway, G. 2000. Genetically modified crops: risks and promise.

Corrado, M., (1989), The Greening Consumer in Britain, MORI, London

Corrado, M., (1997), Green Behaviour – Sustainable Trends, Sustainable Lives?, MORI, london, accessed via countries. Manila, Asian Development Bank 33p.

Cosmetics, Perfume, & Hygiene in Ancient Egypt. Available online: https://www.ancient.eu/article/1061/cosmetics-perfume--hygiene-in-ancient-egypt/ (accessed on 4 May 2017).

Davies, Clive. Chief, Design for the Environment Program, Environmental Protection Agency. Interview. March 24, 2009.

Federal Trade Commission, "Sorting Out Green Advertising Claims." http://www.ftc.gov/bcp/edu/pubs/consumer/general/gen02.shtm (March 26, 2009, March 27, 2009)

MSNBC, "Do You Know What's in Your Cleaning Products?" http://today.msnbc.msn.com/id/29663739/ (March 17, 2009)

Ooyen, Carla. Research Manager with Nutrition Business Journal. Personal correspondence. March 19, 2009.

Tekin, Jenn. Marketing Manager with Packaged Facts & SBI. Personal correspondence. March 17, 2009.

University of California - Berkeley. http://berkeley.edu/news/media/releases/2006/05/22_householdchemicals.shtml (March 26, 2009)

U.S. Department of Health and Human Services, Household Products Database.http://householdproducts.nlm.nih.gov/cgi-bin/household/prodtree?prodcat=Inside+the+Home (March 17,

Women's Voices of the Earth, "Household Cleaning Products and Effects on Human Health."http://www.womenandenvironment.org/campaignsandprograms/SafeCleaning/safecleaninghealth (March 17, 2009)

EMONS, W. Credence Goods Monopolists. International Journal of In- dustrial Organization, Vol. 19 (2001), pp. 375-389.

European Union official website: https://ec.europa.eu/info/about-european-commission/contact_en

Feenstra, R.C. "Exact Hedonic Price Indexes," Review of Economics and Statistics 77 (1995): 634-653.

Feenstra, R.C., and J.A. Levinsohn. "Estimating Markups and Market Conduct with Multidimensional Product Attributes," Review of Economic Studies (62 (1995): 19-52.

Forest Stewardship Council: "Principles and criteria for forest stewardship" Document 1.2: <http://www.fscoax.org>

Forsyth, K. 1999. Will consumers pay more for certified wood products? Journal of Forestry 97 (2) : 18-22.

Freeman, A. M III. The Measurement of Environmental and Resource Values. Theory and Methods. Washington D.C.: Resource for the Future, 1993.

Friends of the Earth, 1993. Timber certification and eco-labeling. London, FOE:

Geetha Margret Soundri, "Ecofriendly Antimicrobial Finishing of Textiles Using Natural Extract", Journal of International Academic Research For Multidisciplinary, ISSN: 2320 – 5083, 2014, Vol 2.

Graves, P., J.C. Murdoch, M.A. Thayer, and D. Waldman. "The Robustness of Hedonic Price Estimation: Urban Air Quality," Land Economics 64(1988): 220-233.

Halvorsen, R. and R. Palmquist. "The Interpretation of Dummy Variables in Semilogarithmic Equations." American Economic Review 70:474-75 (1980).

Imhoff, Dan, and Grose, Lynda, and Carra, Roberto., "Organic Cotton Exhibit," Mimeo. Simple Life and distributed the Texas Organic Cotton Marketing Cooperative, O'Donnell, Texas (1996).

Imhoff, Dan. "Growing Pains: Organic Cotton Tests the Fibre of Growers and Manufacturers Alike," reprinted on Simple Life's web page (simplelife.com), but first printed by Farmer to Farmer, December 1995.

Incomplete Consumer Information in Laboratory Markets. Journal of Environmental labeling.

ISO 14020, ISO 14021,ISO 14024,ISO 14025, International Organization for Standardization.

Kennedy, P.E. "Estimation with Correctly Interpreted Dummy Variables in Semilogarithmic Equations," American Economic Review 71: 801 (1981).

Kirchho®, S., (2000), Green Business and Blue Angels.

Kraus, Jeff. Lab Technician at the North Carolina School of Textiles.

Labeling Issues, Policies and Practices Worldwide.

Lamport, L. 1998. The cast of (timber) certifiers: who are they? International J. Ecoforestry 11(4): 118-122.

Large Scale impoverishment of Amazonian forests by logging and fire. 1999.

Lathrop, K.W. and Centner, T.J. 1998. Eco-labeling and ISO 14000: An analysis of US regulatory systems and issues concerning adoption of type II standards. Environmental

Lee, J. et al. 1996. Trade related environmental measures; sizing and comparing impacts.

Lehtonen, Markku. 1997. Criteria in Environmental Labeling: A comparative Analysis on Environmental Criteria in Selected Labeling Schemes. Geneva, UNEP. 148p.

LIEBI, T. Trusting Labels: A Matter of Numbers? Working Paper Uni versity of Bern, No. 0201 (2002).

Lindstrom, T. 1999. Forest Certification: The View from Europe's NIPFs. Journal of Forestry 97(3): 25-31. London

Losey, J.E., Rayor, L.S. & Carter, M.E. 1999. Transgenic pollen harms monarch larvae. Nature 399 20 May): p.214.

Management 22 (2) : 163-172.

Mattoo, A. and H. V. Singh, (1994), Eco-Labelling: Policy Considera-Michaels, R. G., and V. K. Smith. "Market Segmentation And Valuing Amenities With Hedonic Models: The Case Of Hazardous Waste Sites," Journal of Urban Economics, 1990 28(2), 223-242.

Nicholson-Lord, D., (1993) 'Tis the Season to be Green, The Independent, 20 December

Nuttall, N., (1993), Shoppers can cross green products off their lists, The Times, 3 July

OCDE/GD(97)105. Paris, OECD. 81p.

OECD. "Ec-labelling: Actual Effects of Selected Programmes," OCDE/GD (97) 105, 1997, Paris. (available on line at http://www.oecd.org/env/eco/books.htm#trademono)

OECD. 1997a. Case study on eco-labeling schemes. Paris, OECD (30 Dec):

OECD. 1997b. Eco-labeling: Actual Effects of Selected Programs.

Osborne, L. "Market Structure, Hedonic Models, and the Valuation of Environmental Amenities." Unpublished Ph.D. dissertation. North Carolina State University, 1995.

Osborne, L., and V. K. Smith. "Environmental Amenities, Product Differentiation, and market Power," Mimeo, 1997.

Ozanne, L.K. and Vlosky, R.P. 1996. Wood products environmental certification: the United States perspective". Forestry Chronicle 72 (2) : 157-165.

Palmquist, R. B., F. M. Roka, and T.Vukina. "Hog Operations, Environmental Effects, and Residential Property Values," Land Economics 73(1), (1997): 114-24.

Palmquist, R.B. "Hedonic Methods," in J.B Braden and C.D. Kolstad, eds. Measuring the Demand for Environmental Improvement. Amsterdam, NL: Elsevier, 1991.

Pento, T. 1997. Implementation of Public Green Procurement Programs (22-31) in Greener Purchasing: Opportunities and Innovations. Sheffield, Greenleaf Publ. 325 p.

Perloff, J. "Industrial Organization Lecture Notes," Mimeo. University of California at Berkeley (1985).

Plant, C. and Plant, J. 1991. Green business: hope or hoax? Philadelphia, New Society Publishers 136 p.

Polak, J. and Bergholm, K. 1997. Eco-labeling and trade: a cooperative approach (Jan.): Policy in a Green Market. Environmental and Resource Economics 22, 419-

Poore, M.E.D. et al. 1989. No timber without trees. London, Earthscan. 352p.

Raff, D. M.G., and M. Trajtenberg. "Quality-Adjusted Prices for the American Automobile Industry: 1906-1940." NBER Working Paper Series, Working Paper No. 5035, February 1995.

Roberts, J. T. 1998. Emerging global environment standards: prospects and perils. Journal of Developing Societies 14 (1): 144-163.

Rosen, S., "Hedonic Prices and Implicit Markets: Product Differentiation in Pure Competition." Journal of Political Economy. 82: 34-55 (1974).

Ross, B. 1997. Eco-friendly procurement training course for UN HCR. : 126 p.

Ryan, S., and Skipworth, M., (1993), Consumers turn their backs on green revolution, The Times, 4 April

Salzman, J. 1997. Informing the Green Consumer: The Debate over the Use and Abuse of Environmental Labels. Journal of Industrial Ecology 1 (2): 11-22.

Sanders, W. 1997. Environmentally Preferable Purchasing: The US Experience (946-960) in Greener Purchasing: Opportunities and Innovations. Sheffield, Greenleaf Publ. 325p.

Sayre, D. 1996. Inside ISO 14000: The competitive advantage of environmental management. Delray Beach FL., St. Lucie Press. 232p.

SHAPIRO, C. Premiums for High Quality Products as Returns to Reputa- tion. Quarterly Journal of Economics, Vol. 98, No. 4 (1983), pp. 659-680.

Stillwell, M. and van Dyke, B. 1999. An activists handbook on genetically modified organisms and the WTO. Washington DC., The Consumer's Choice Council: 20 p.

Semenzato, A.; Costantini, A.; Meloni, M.; Maramaldi, G.; Meneghin, M.; Baratto, G. Formulating O/W Emulsions with Plant-Based Actives: A Stability Challenge for an Eective Product. Cosmetics 2018, 5, 59.

Teisl, M. F., B. Roe, and R. L. Hicks. "Can Eco-labels tune a market? Evidence from dolphin-safe labeling," Presented paper at the 1997 American Agricultural Economics Association Meetings, Toronto.

THE GERSEN, C. Psychological Determinants of Paying Attention to Eco- Labels in Purchase Decisions: Model Development and Multinational Vali- dation. Journal of Consumer Policy, Vol. 23, No. 4 (2000), pp. 285-313.

Tibor, T. and Feldman, I. 1995. ISO 14000: a guide to the new environmental management standards. Burr Ridge Ill., Irwin Professional Publ. 250 p.

Torre, I. de la, & Batker, D. K. (n.d.) 1999-2000. Prawn to trade: prawn to consume. Graham WA., Industrial Shrimp Action Network (isatorre@seanet.com), [and] Asia –Pacific Townsend, M. 1998. Making things greener: motivations and influences in the greening of manufacturing. Aldershot, England, Ashgate Publisher. 203p.

U.S. Energy Information Administration, What is U.S. Electricity Generation by Energy Source?, Retrieved From: https://www.eia.gov/tools/faqs/faq.php?id=427&t=3

U.S. Energy Information Administration, Biomass Explained, Retrieved From: https://www.eia.gov/energyexplained/?page=biomass_home

U.S. Environmental Protection Agency. National Water Quality Fact Inventory: 1990 Report to Congress. EPA 503-9-92-006, Apr. 1992.

UK Eco-labelling Board website, accessed via http://www.ecosite.co.uk/Ecolabel-UK/

US Environmental Protection Agency (EPA742-R-99-001): 40 p. <www.epa.gov/opptintr/epp>

US EPA, 1993. Determinants of effectiveness for environmental certification and labeling programs. Washington, D.C., US Environmental Protect

US EPA, 1993. Status report on the use of environmental labels worldwide. Washington, D.C., US Environmental Protection Agency (742-R-93-001 September).

US EPA, 1993. The use of life-cycle assessment in environmental labeling. Washington, D.C., US Environmental Protection Agency (742-R-93-003 September).

US EPA, 1998. Environmental labeling: issues, policies, and practices worldwide. Washington DC., Environmental Protection Agency, Pollution Prevention Division Prepared by Abt

US EPA, 1999. Comprehensive procurement guidelines (CPG) program. Washington, D.C., US Environmental Protection Agency: <www.epa.gov/cpg>

US EPA, 1999. Environmentally preferable purchasing program: Private sector pioneers: How companies are incorporating environmentally preferable purchases. Washington, D.C.,

USG, 1993. Federal acquisition, recycling, and waste prevention. Washington DC., Executive Order: (20 October).

USG, 1998. Greening the government through waste prevention, recycling, and federal acquisition. Washington, D.C., Executive Order 13101 (September).

Kijjoa, A.; Sawangwong, P. Drugs and Cosmetics from the Sea. Mar. Drugs 2004, 2, 73–82. [CrossRef]

Wang, J.; Pan, L.; Wu, S.; Lu, L.; Xu, Y.; Zhu, Y.; Guo, M.; Zhuang, S. Recent Advances on Endocrine Disrupting Eects of UV Filters. Int. J. Environ. Res. Public Health 2016, 13, 782.

Bilal, A.I.; Tilahun, Z.; Shimels, T.; Gelan, Y.B.; Osman, E.D. Cosmetics Utilization Practice in Jigjiga Town, Eastern Ethiopia: A Community Based Cross-Sectional Study. Cosmetics 2016, 3, 40.

Ting, C.T.; Hsieh, C.M.; Chang, H.-P.; Chen, H.-S. Environmental Consciousness and Green Customer Behavior: The Moderating Roles of Incentive Mechanisms. Sustainability 2019, 11, 819.

Chen, K.; Deng, T. Research on the Green Purchase Intentions from the Perspective of Product Knowledge. Sustainability 2016, 8, 943.

Wang, H.; Ma, B.; Bai, R. How Does Green Product Knowledge Eectively Promote Green Purchase Intention? Sustainability 2019, 11, 1193.

Nguyen, T.T.H.; Yang, Z.; Nguyen, N.; Johnson, L.W.; Cao, T.K. Greenwash and Green Purchase Intention: The Mediating Role of Green Skepticism. Sustainability 2019, 11, 2653.

Cinelli, P.; Coltelli, M.B.; Signori, F.; Morganti, P.; Lazzeri, A. Cosmetic Packaging to Save the Environment: Future Perspectives. Cosmetics 2019, 6, 26.

Eixarch, H.; Wyness, L.; Siband, M. The Regulation of Personalized Cosmetics in the EU. Cosmetics 2019, 6, 29.

CANADA BRONZE BEAVER BADGE

Participate in our Online Classes to earn these exclusive digital badges!
www.toptenaward.org

Design & Development by:

Tara Asadi

CANADA GOLD BEAVER BADGE

Participate in our Online Classes to earn these exclusive digital badges!

Design & Development by:

Tara Asadi

Environmental Lifestyle Guide

For Grade 9

For Grade 10

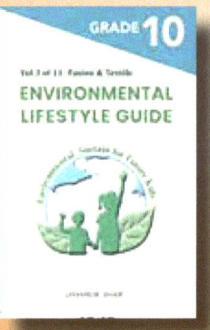
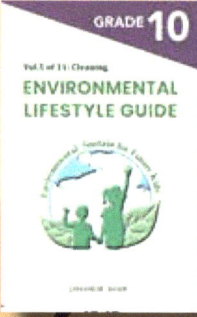
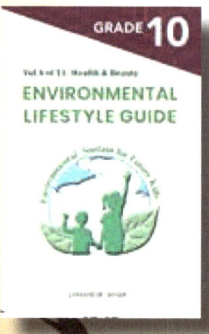

Plus Online Certification Tests via:
https://toptenaward.org

Standard Text Books

For Grade 11

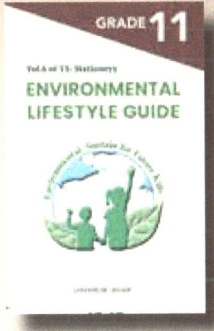 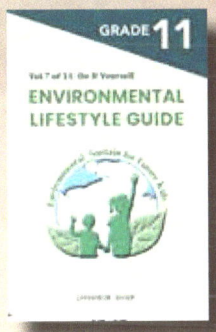 

For Grade 12

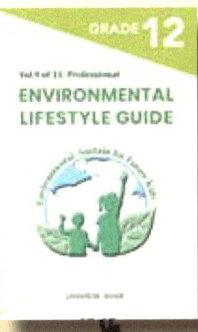 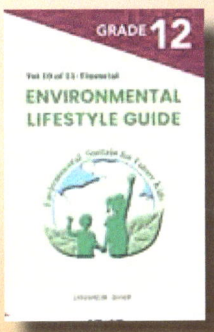 

**Environmental Lifestyle Guide
Standard Text Book**
For Students Grade 9 to 12
Available in more than
39,000 Bookstores
all over the globe.
https://ecofriendlyeducation.com

Cooperation by:
Top Ten Award International Network
&
Environmental Sustain for Future Kids